What Do You Hear?

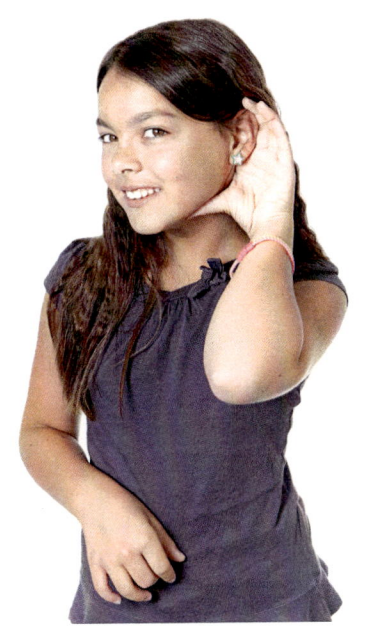

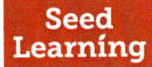
Seed Learning

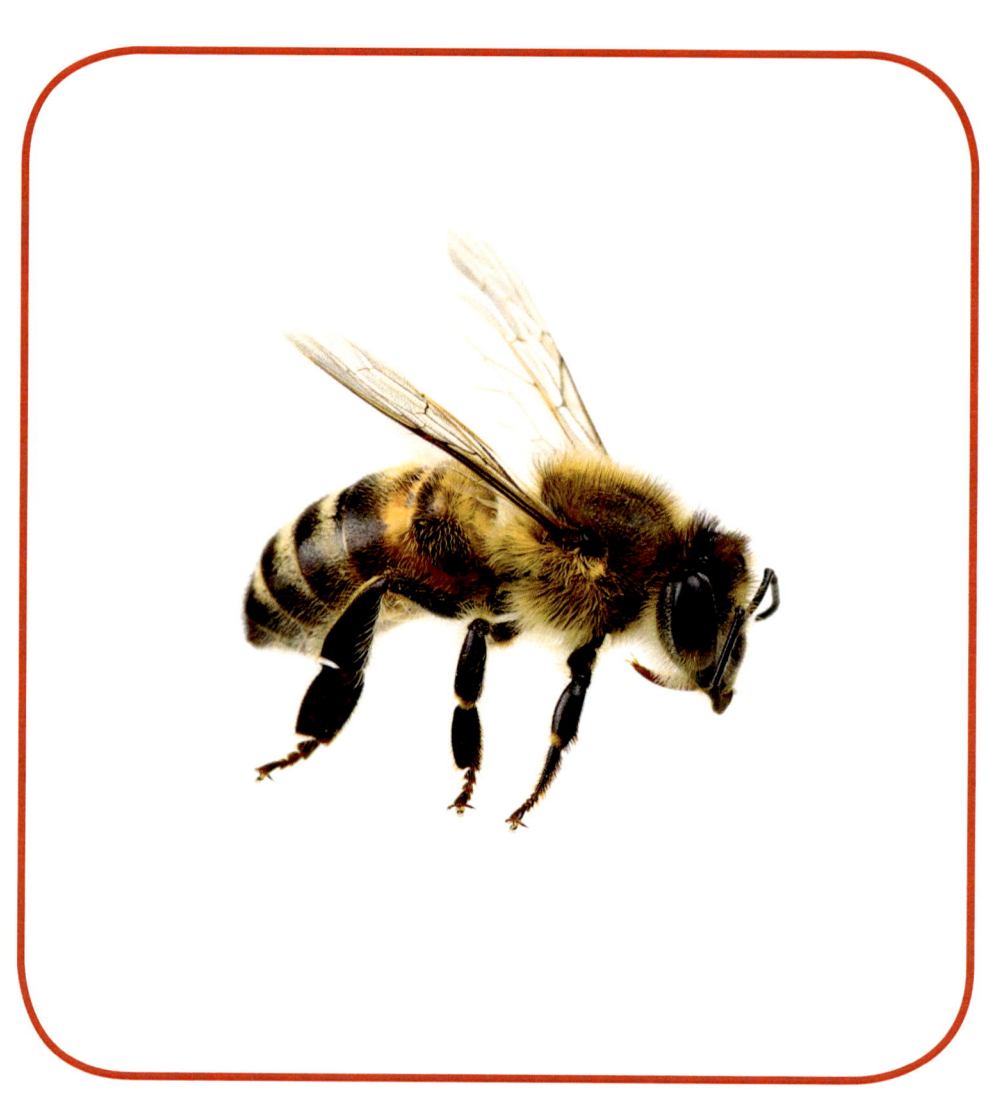

bee

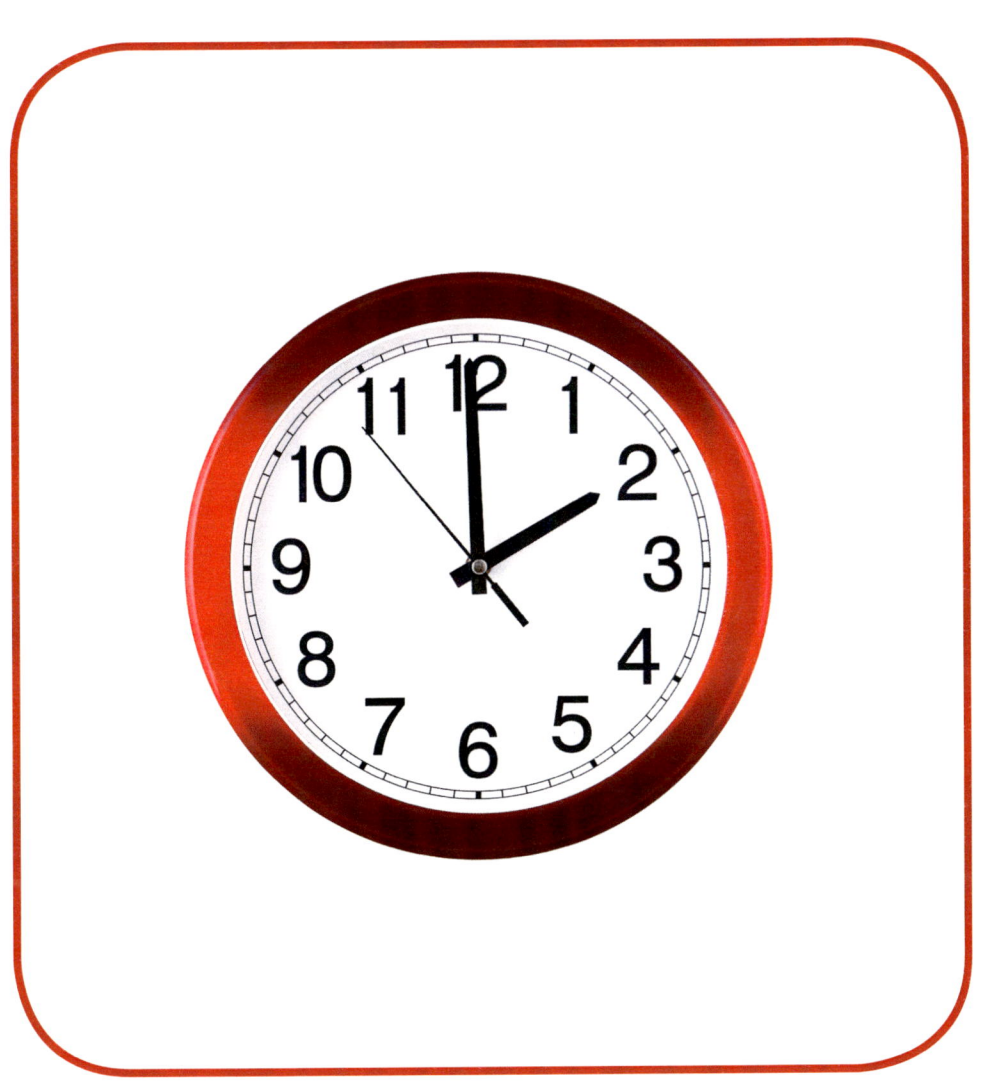

clock

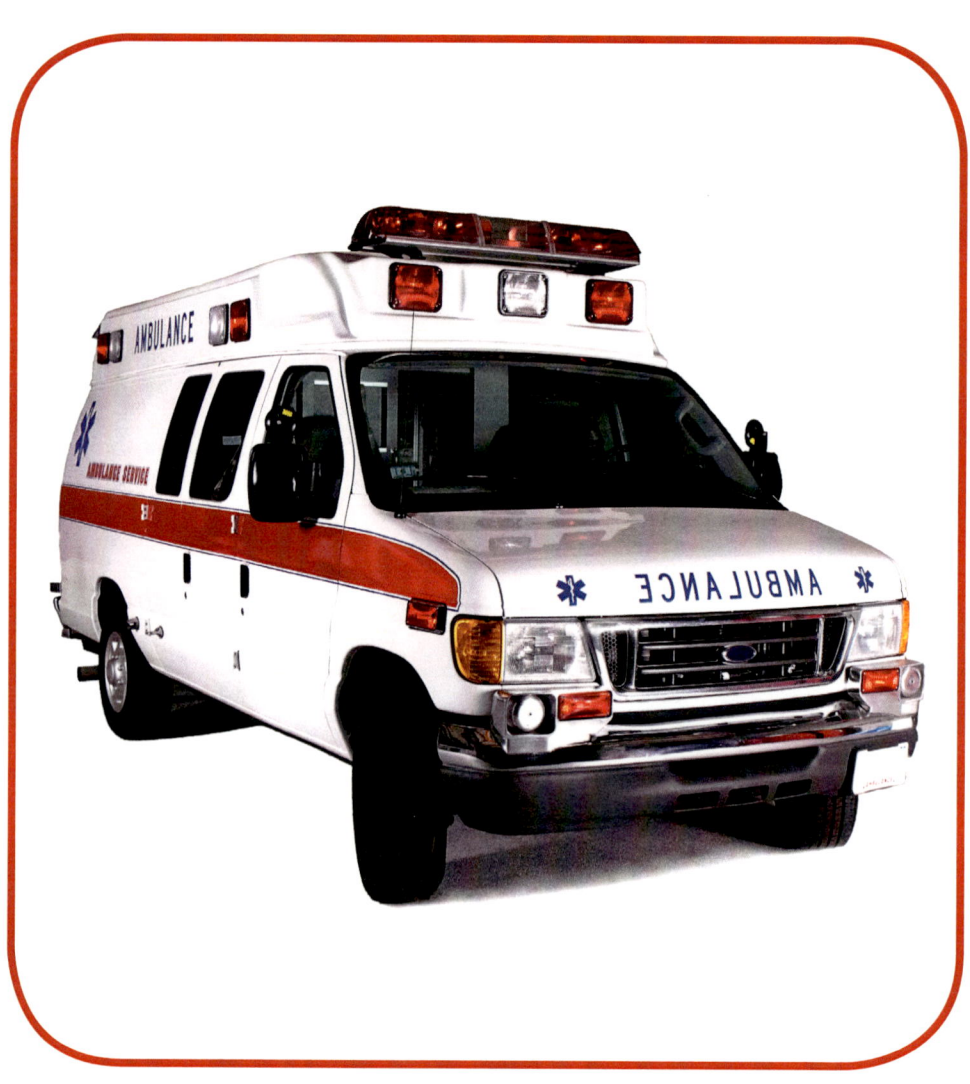

ambulance

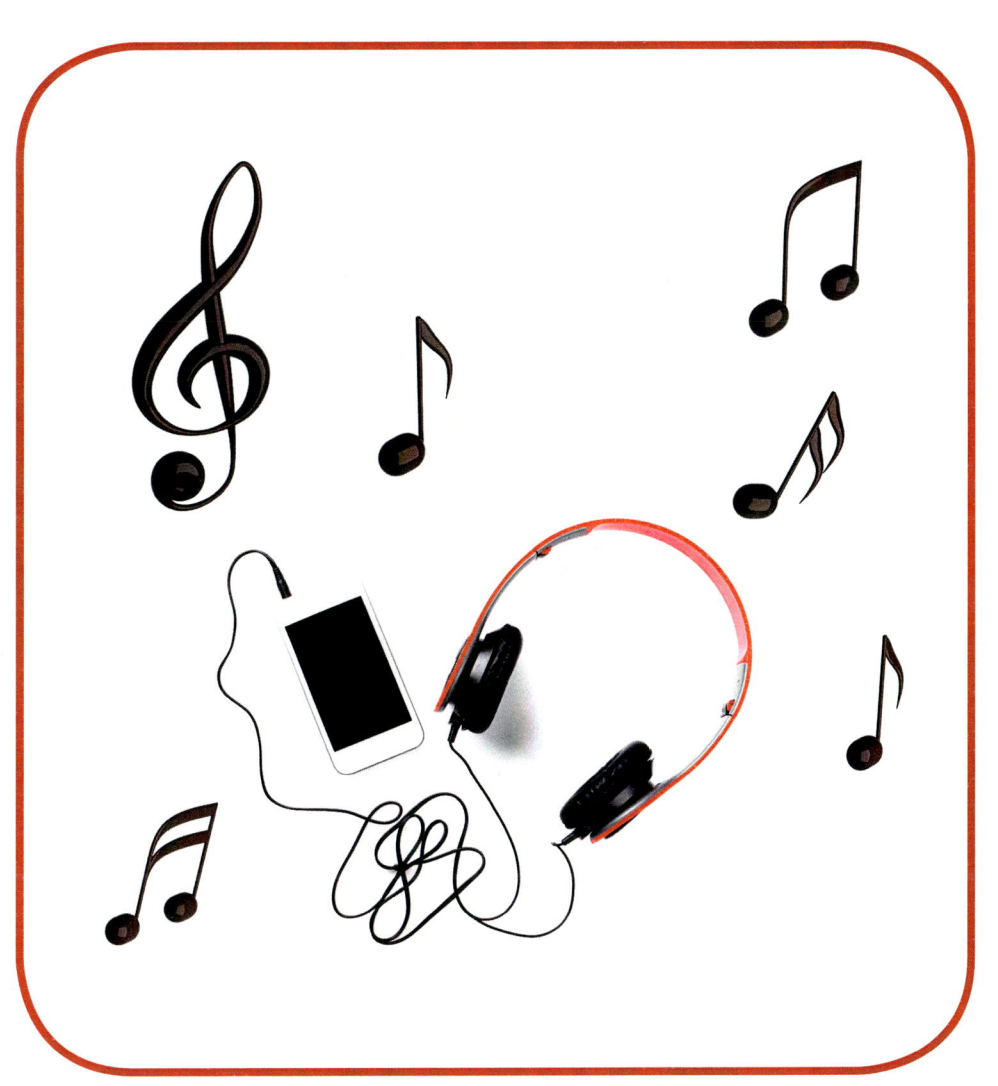

music

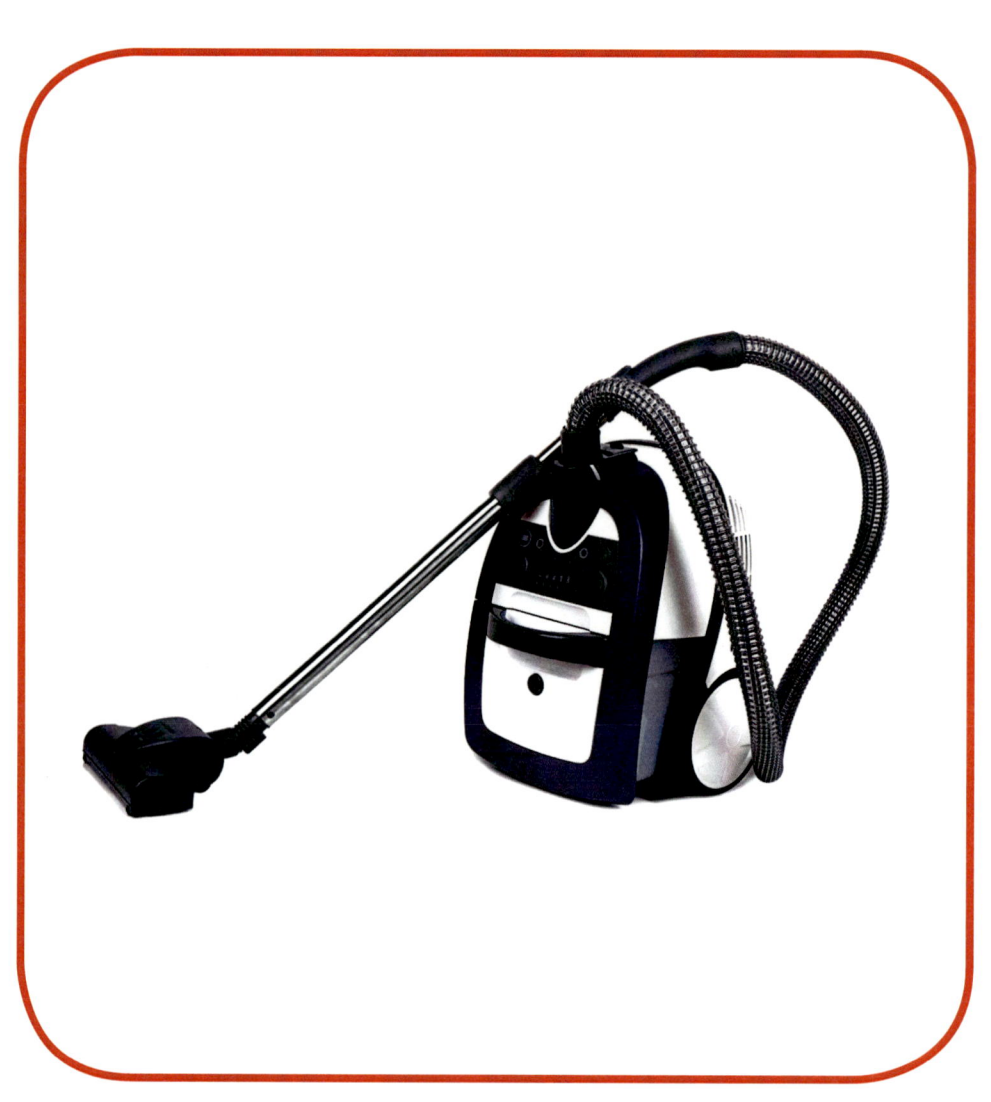

vacuum

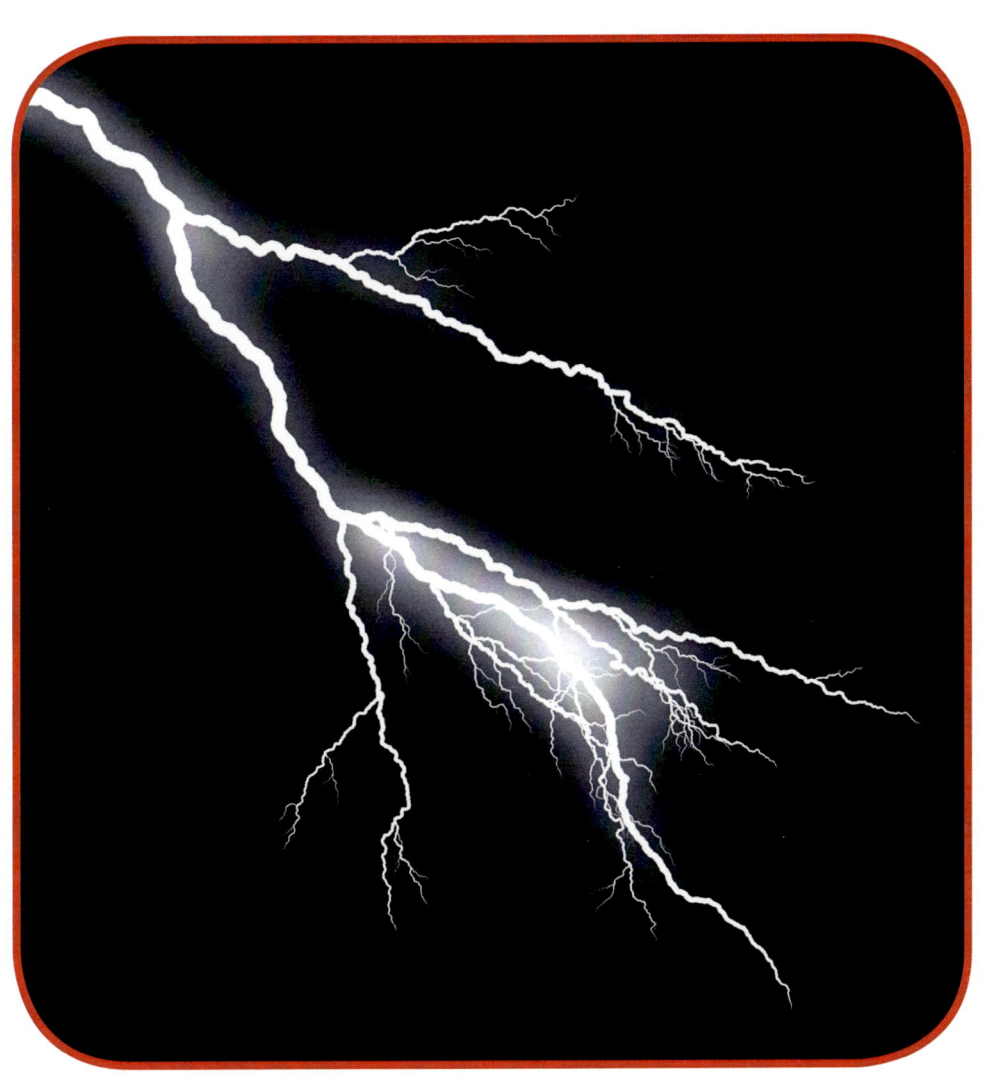

thunder

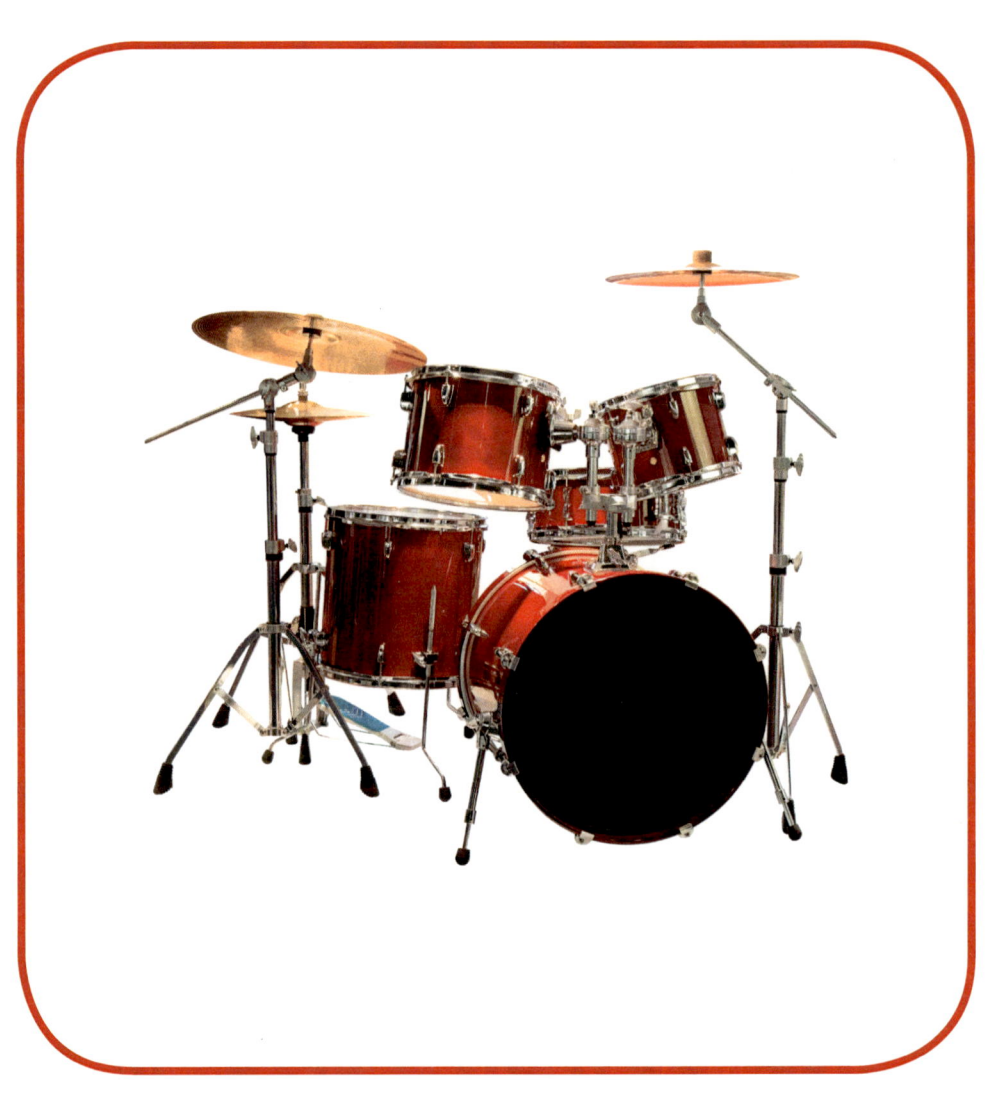

drums

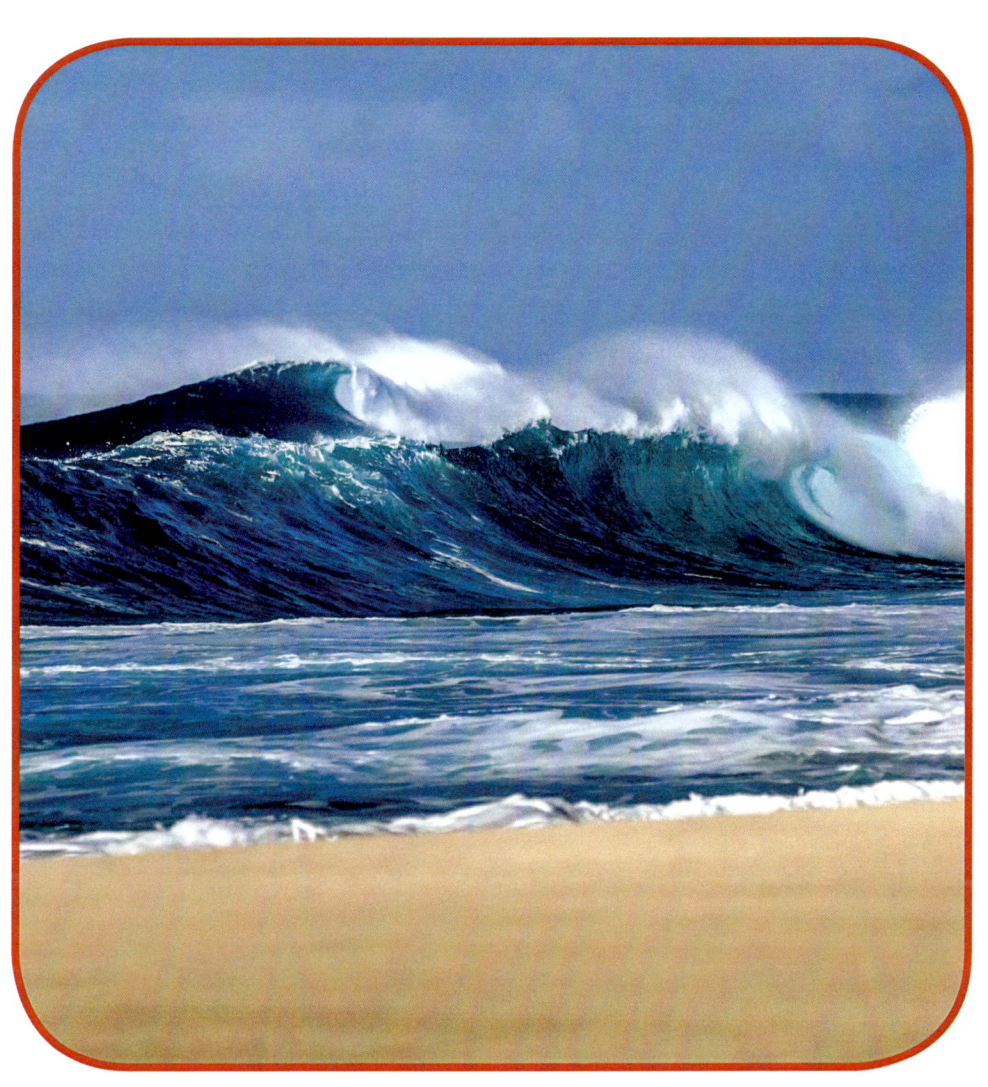

waves

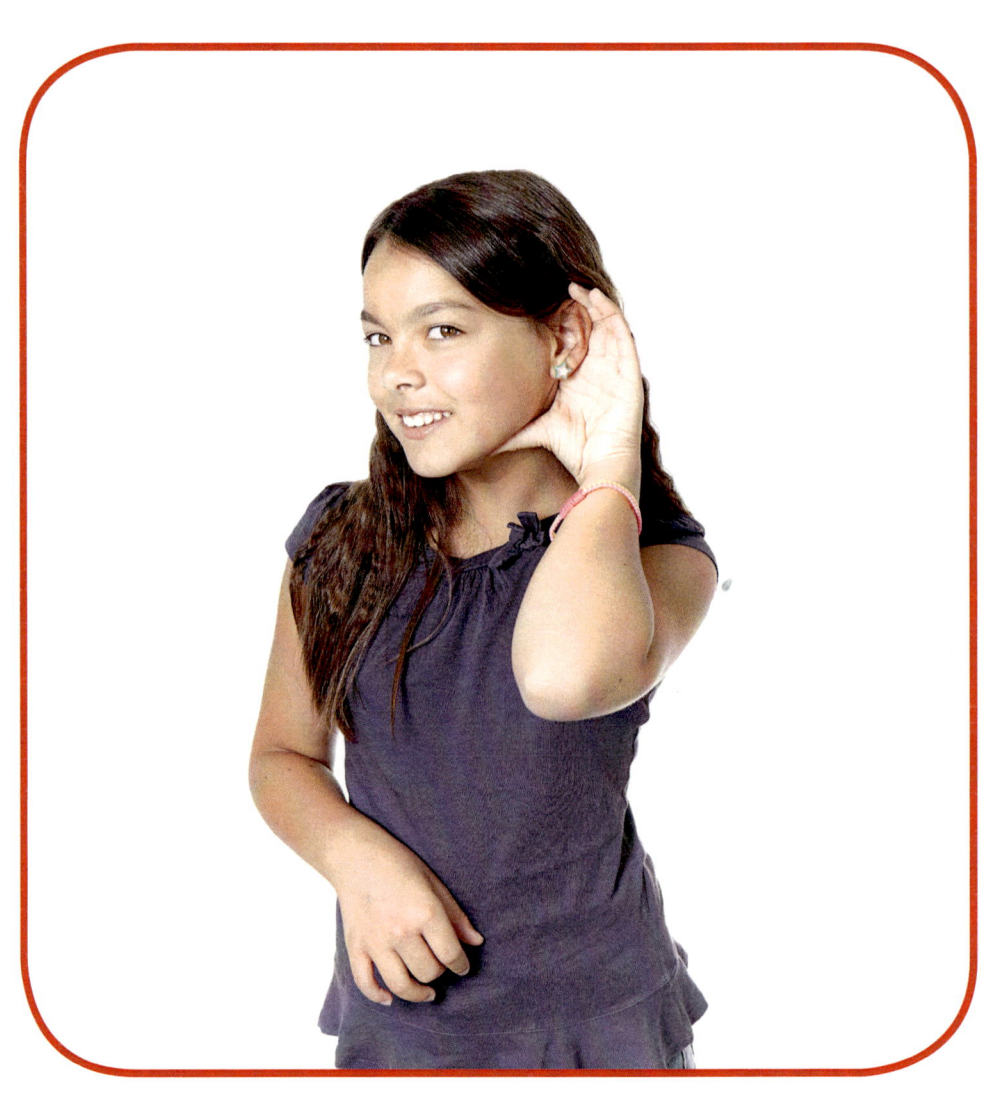

What do you hear?

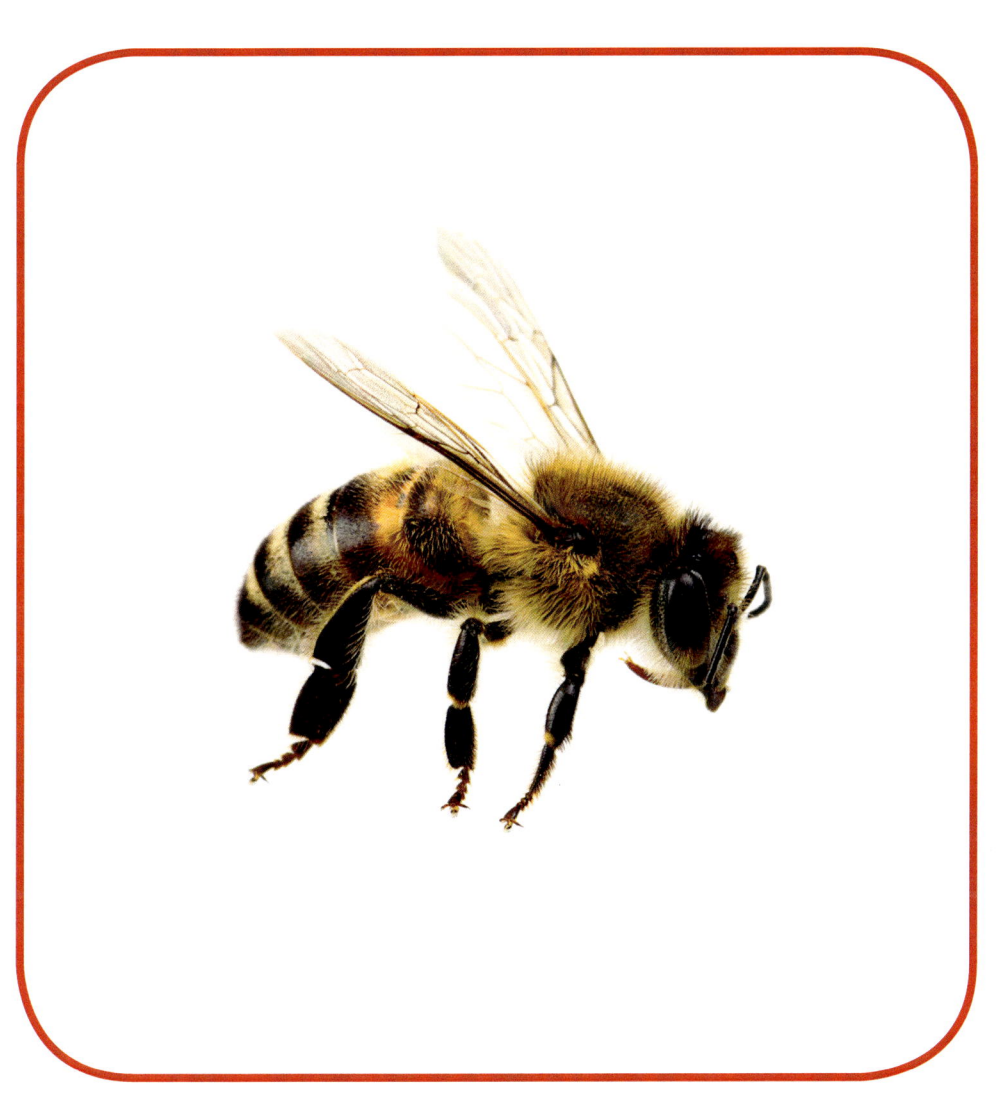

I hear a bee.

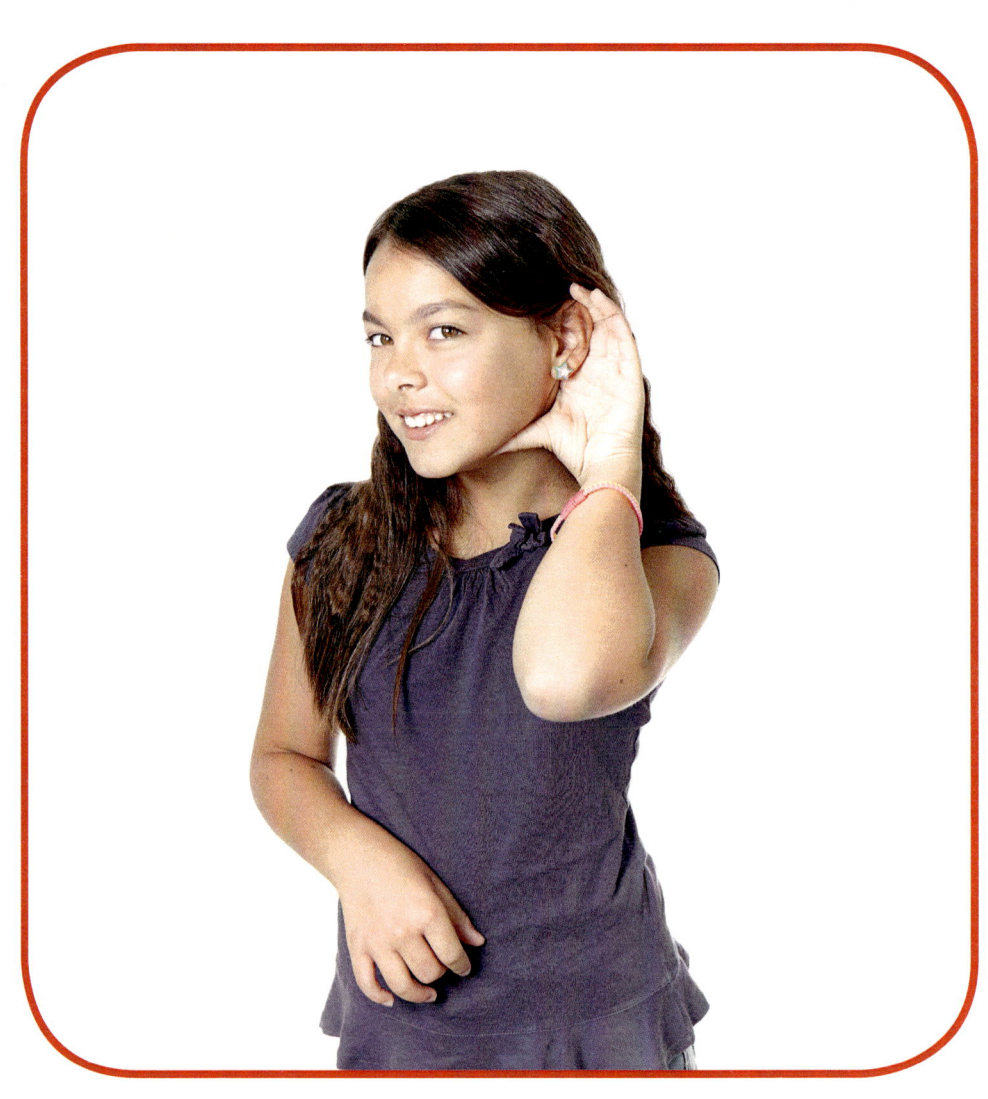

What do you hear?

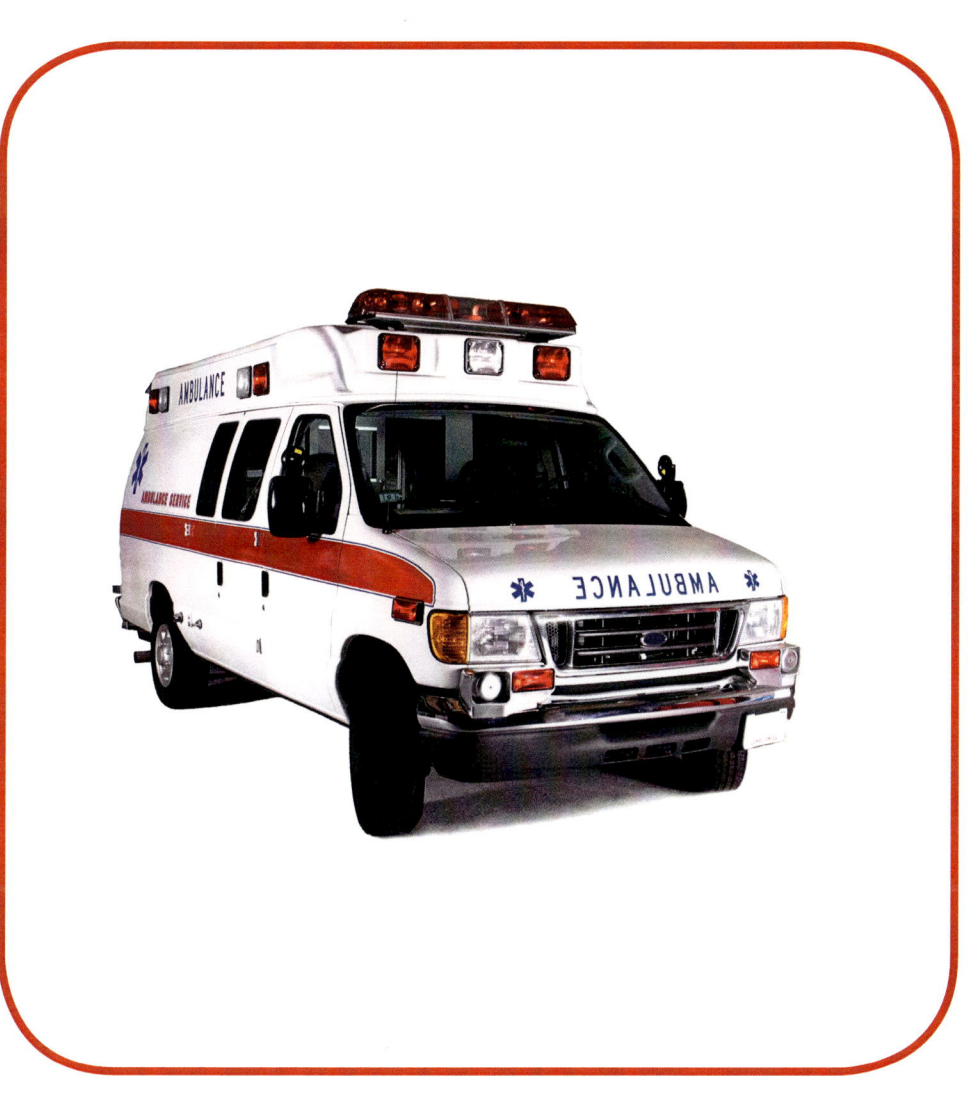

I hear an
ambulance.

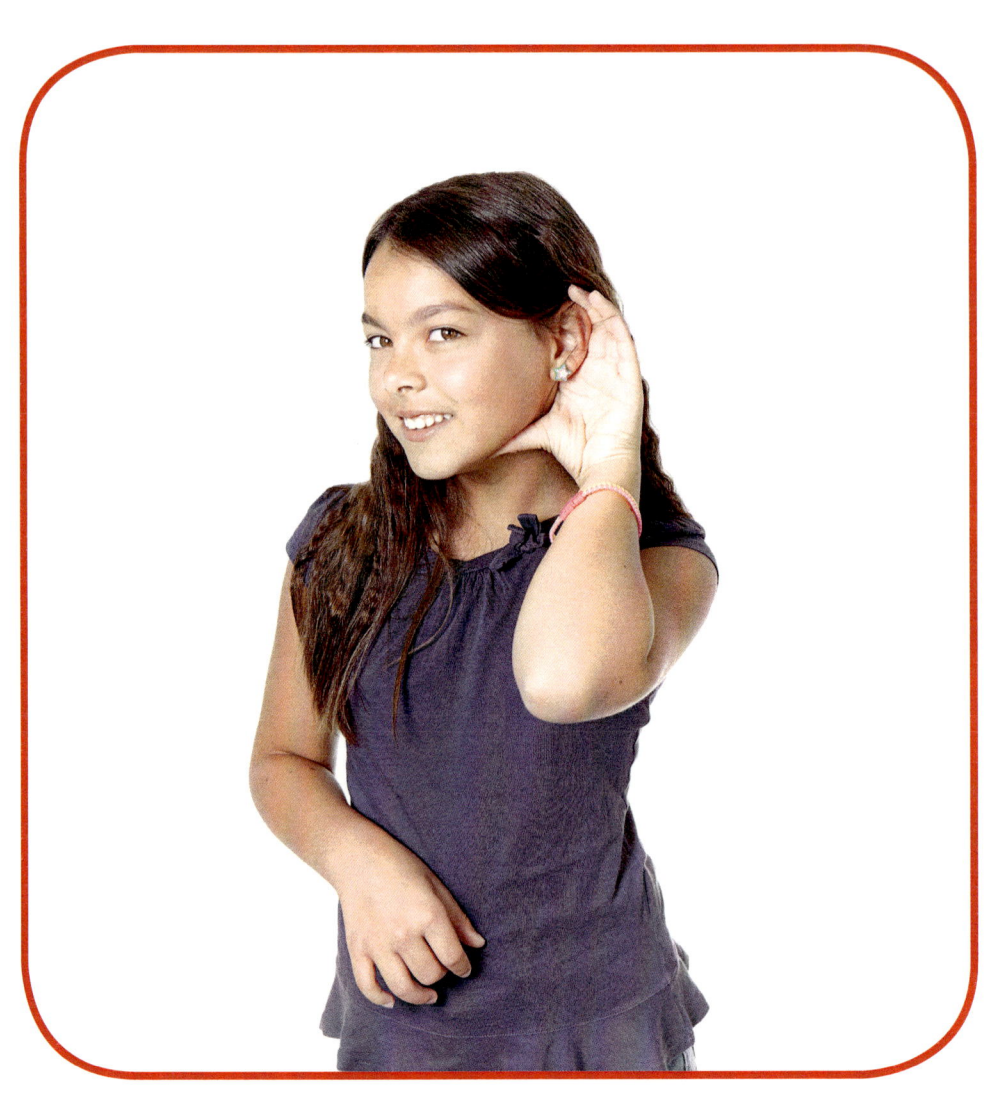

What do you hear?

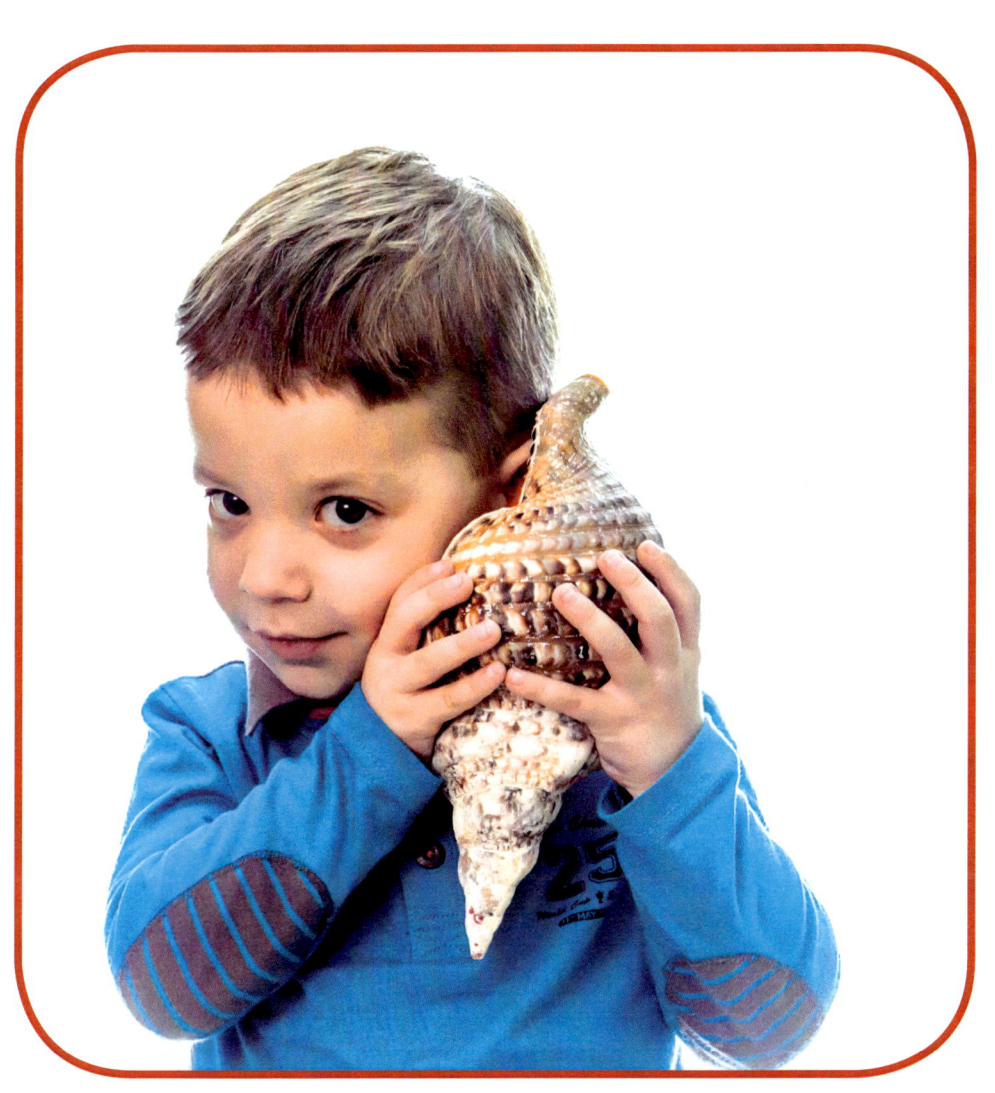

I hear waves.

Let's learn more about India.

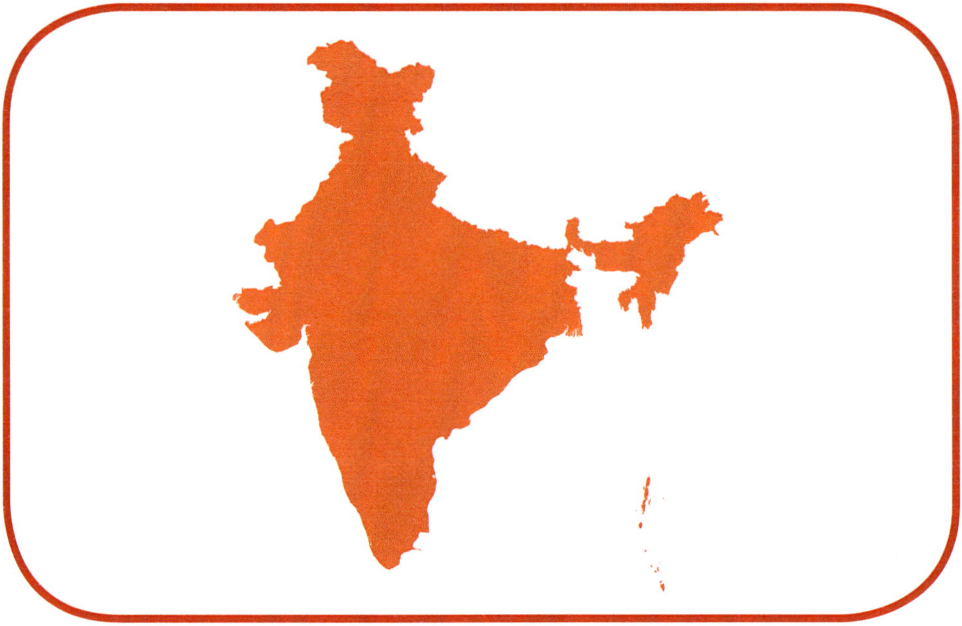

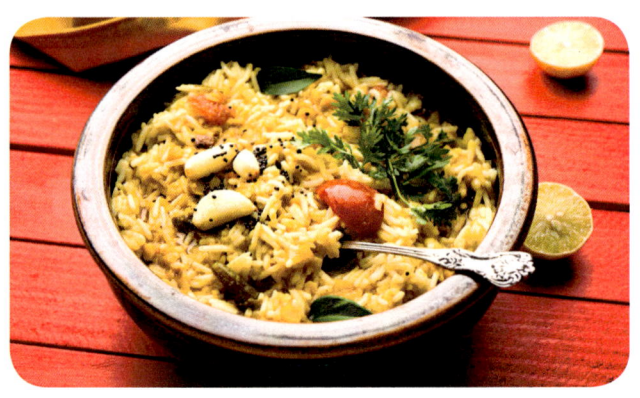

Khichdi